Publisher: Credible Math, LLC.

Author: Deborah Reynolds

Photo Images: istock.com

Any internet websites printed are used as resources only. The mention of these websites should not be considered an endorsement by the author or Credible Math, LLC and we do not vouch for the content of these websites over the life of this book.

Copyright: 2012 by Deborah Reynolds. Revised Second Edition: 2019. All rights reserved.

No part of this book may be reproduced or transmitted in any form or by any means, mechanical, electronic, including recording and photocopying, or by any information storage or retrieval system, without the prior written approval of Deborah Reynolds unless such copying is expressly permitted by federal copyright law. Address all inquiries to Credible Math LLC, 20 Baltimore Avenue, Piscataway, NJ. 08854.

Email: dreynolds@crediblemath.com.

Printed in the USA.

A Word from the Author

The Young Entrepreneurs Financial Literacy Handbook was written to support a performance based financial literacy program developed by **CREDIBLE MATH, LLC**. It can be designed around an ongoing business. In weekly seminars, students are taught basic entrepreneurship, finance, and accounting skills needed to operate a business. The business could be a school store, concession stand, or kiosk which acts as a learning laboratory. Students collect and analyze data on information such as sales and inventory to prepare financial statements. Data may also be obtained from neighborhood businesses. Local entrepreneurs are encouraged to participate.

Each topic begins with **objectives** for student learning. There is an **essential question** which does not have a right or wrong answer, but gives the students something to think about as they go through the topic.

The **warm-up** is a review of the previous topic. **Topic highlights** provide key information on each topic along with definitions. The **activities and assessments** were written to align with the Common Core State Standards (CCSS). These are the standards used to assess student achievement from grades kindergarten through twelve. Each topic ends with a **wrap-up** activity which summarizes the information students should have learned while covering the topic.

TABLE OF CONTENTS

Topic 1	Recognizing Business Opportunities	pg.01
Topic 2	Team Building	pg.08
Topic 3	Managing Business Finances	pg.18
Topic 4	Banking Services	pg.24
Topic 5	Credit	pg.31
Topic 6	Saving and Investing	pg.36
Topic 7	The Business Plan	pg.46
Topic 8	Marketing	pg.58

Appendices: pg.59

Appendix A: Personal Monthly Budget

Appendix B: Sample Consolidated Balance Sheet

Appendix C: Sample Monthly Income Statement

Appendix D: Sample Monthly Statement of Cash Flows

TOPIC 1

RECOGNIZING BUSINESS OPPORTUNITIES

TOPIC 1: RECOGNIZING BUSINESS OPPORTUNITIES

OBJECTIVES: Students will be able to:

- Identify elements of creative thinking
- Discuss meaning of "thinking out of the box."
- Investigate places to look for inspiration
- Identify and explore current business trends
- Identify famous entrepreneurs and what factors contributed to their success.

ESSENTIAL QUESTION: How does thinking creatively support business opportunities?

TOPIC 1 HIGHLIGHTS

The dictionary defines opportunity as a favorable or promising combination of circumstances which provide a good chance for advancement or progress. In business an opportunity has commercial value. We are always looking for opportunities to expand our business by increasing sales and profits. We usually do this by making improvements on existing products and services. We have to think about the needs of our customers. What improvements can be made to increase our customer base and make the company a leader in its industry?

To take advantage of opportunity, we must learn to think creatively. When we think creatively, we use our imagination to rise above or transcend traditional ideas, methods, patterns, rules, products, relationships, etc., and produce something new. This process is also referred to as "thinking out of the box." We also use a technique called "brainstorming", where ideas are given without being judged as good or bad, right or wrong.

The elements of creativity are connection, discovery, invention, and application. We connect things that are usually not connected. Cookie dough and ice cream is an example of this process.

In order to get inspired to think creatively, you must first stop and observe the world around you. Look at people when you are in the mall, in a park, and on vacation.

Describe the personal characteristics of the people you encounter. These characteristics are called **demographics** and include gender, race, culture, income, education, and ethnicity. Also read newspapers and magazines to get ideas. Finally, use the internet.

What is an entrepreneur?

An **entrepreneur** is a person who creates, organizes, operates, and owns a business. They assume the financial risk and responsibilities in starting and running a new business or **venture**. To start a business requires many skills which will be explored in this handbook.

Entrepreneurship is the process of identifying a potential business, finding and testing it on potential customers, and obtaining the financing to start the business.

To help develop new business opportunities, you must identify current business trends. The biggest trends today are e-business and e-commerce which use the internet. Almost every field including retail sales, education, finance, and publishing does business on the internet. Also, social media businesses such as fashion and entertainment blogs have proved to be financially successful. Developing medical, dating, and game apps is popular. Service businesses such as fitness centers, pet grooming, food catering, and wedding planning are on the rise. Many new entrepreneurs choose **franchising** when starting their own business. When you purchase a franchise, you become the owner of an outpost of a larger Steamer, and Comfort Inn are examples of franchise businesses. When purchasing a franchise you purchase a territory and franchisor's business system, which includes accounting, advertising, and procedures.

Finally, if we look at the lives of some famous entrepreneurs such as Jeff Bezos (Amazon), Elon Musk (Tesla and SpaceX), Steven Jobs (Apple Inc.), Bill Gates (Microsoft), Tyler Perry (Tyler Perry Studios), Oprah Winfrey (OWN), Warren Buffett (Berkshire Hathaway), and Mark Zuckerberg (Facebook), we find that their environments and interest provided the inspiration for their success.

ACTIVITIES/ASSESSMENTS:

1. Identify two additional current business trends and their products. Write a short paragraph on each and give an oral presentation. Work with a partner on this activity.

2. Use the elements of creative thinking, brainstorming, and demographics to create new school store items to sell. Students work in small groups and compete to see which group can come up with the most sellable new items.

3. Use the internet to identify 5 e-businesses and give their web addresses.

4. Identify and research a business franchise. Describe the business and start up costs needed. Use the search engine franchise.org to help get information.

5. Choose two famous entrepreneurs and determine what factors inspired their success. Present your results by writing a short paragraph.

WRAP-UP: Students will present a 2 minute commercial summarizing this lesson.

TOPIC 2

TEAM BUILDING

TOPIC 2: TEAM BUILDING

OBJECTIVES: Students will be able to:

- Identify the key characteristics of a good team
- Develop interviewing skills
- Define and analyze factors influencing wages

ESSENTIAL QUESTION: How does choosing a good team impact the success of a business?

WARM-UP: List the elements of creative thinking

TOPIC 2 HIGHLIGHTS

1. Team building/Teamwork

Team building is essential to the success of operating a business. A **team** consists of two or more people organized to work together to accomplish a task or reach a common goal. Teams bring together the particular skills and knowledge of its members. Working in the school concession stand uses the concept of work teams which are groups of students assigned to an event. The event can be an athletic event or festival. Working in the school store also uses the work team concept. However this is a daily operation at a permanent location. Each person on the team has a responsibility. The responsibility could be counting inventory; displaying inventory; preparing food; cleaning and maintenance; serving customers; handling money; or keeping financial records. There should also be a manager to make sure all tasks are completed in a timely manner.

The following are some general characteristics of a good team:

- A clear goal or mission which everyone accepts
- Willing participation by every member
- Open and relaxed communication between members
- Clear understanding of work assignments
- Resolve problems on a timely basis
- Use listening skills by focusing on the speaker
- Recognize that disagreements will arise, but remain respectful of each other.
- Regular evaluation of the team's performance to see if work can be done better

2. Interviewing

Before being considered for any job, the job seeker must complete a job application and a job interview. For many jobs there may be several stages until an actual face to face interview. This is especially true for professional jobs and applications online. The company may receive thousands of applications. To narrow the number of applicants the first interview may be via phone. There may be a second interview via Skype or FaceTime. The final job interview enables the employer to have face to face contact to see if the applicant fits into the culture of a particular workplace. The interview also allows the applicant to tell why they are the best person for the job. The following are guidelines for a successful interview:

- Dress appropriately, good grooming and hygiene matter. Check your body language. Keep your hands in your lap. Do not sit back with your arms folded.

- Research the company. You should know such things as what they produce and who their competitors are.
- Be courteous and polite.
- Ask questions to the interviewer about job responsibilities and training
- Be prepared to answer common interview questions such as:

    a. Why do you want this job?

    b. Can you tell us something about yourself?

    c. What is your greatest strength?

After the interview, thank the interviewer for their time and effort.

3. Factors influencing wages

A **wage** is the amount of money one receives for every hour worked. Thus the wage is expressed as a rate- $9.00/hr, or $8.75 per hour. A **pay** or **total earnings** is the amount received for a pay period. The period could be weekly, biweekly, twice a month, or monthly. The hours worked are recorded on a time sheet and the pay is shown on a payroll stub.

Example: Anthony worked 35 hours this week and earns $9.50 per hour. What are his total earnings?

Answer: $9.50 x 35 = $332.50

Thus, wages or pay is influenced by the hourly rate and the hours worked.

Gross pay is the total amount earned during a pay period. Net pay(take-home pay) is the amount left after federal, state, local taxes, social security(FICA), and disability insurance(SDI) are deducted from the gross pay.

ACTIVITIES/ASSESSMENTS

1. Identify additional characteristics you desire in a good team member.

2. Create a poster on all the characteristics of a good team member.

3. Students practice job interviewing by pairing off. One person will represent the employer and the other will play the job applicant. They will later reverse roles. If possible this activity should be videotaped.

4. Complete the time card for several employees, given the hours worked daily.

TIME CARD

Employee #

Employee Name:

Week Ending_____ 20___

	A.M.		P.M.		Hours
	In	Out	In	Out	Worked
Mon.					
Tues.					
Wed.					
Thurs.					
Fri.					
Sat.					
Sun.					

5. Complete the earnings portion of the following pay stub given:

    Regular hours -40

    Overtime hours -6

    Regular pay rate -$8.50

    Overtime rate – time and a half (1.5 x regular rate)

PAY STUB

EARNINGS

WEEK ENDING	PAY RATE	REGULAR PAY	OVER TIME HOURS	REGULAR PAY	OVER TIME PAY	GROSS PAY	

DEDUCTIONS

FICA	FWT	STATE TAX	LOCAL TAX	SDI	OTHER	TOTAL DEDUCTIONS	NET PAY

WRAP-UP

Present pros and cons why a potential employer should be able to view your Facebook, Twitter, or Instagram accounts.

TOPIC 3

MANAGING BUSINESS FINANCES

TOPIC 3: MANAGING BUSINESS FINANCES

Objectives: *Students will be able to:*

- *Develop short, intermediate, and long term goals*

- *Distinguish income from expense items*

- *Prepare a budget*

- *Become familiar with various types of financial statements*

- Collect data necessary to complete a spreadsheet

- Prepare an income, cash flow, and balance sheet using monthly data collected from a business such as the school store.

ESSENTIAL QUESTION: How is data used to forecast business operations?

WARM-UP:

- Identify three guidelines for a successful job interview.
- Explain the difference between gross pay and net pay.

TOPIC 3 HIGHTLIGHTS

GOALS – Short Term, Intermediate, and Long Term

Goals unlike dreams have a specific time limit. **Goals** are objectives that we work towards achieving. They may be **short term goals** which can be achieved in less than three months. Examples are exercise 20 minutes daily for a month; save money for an upcoming concert ticket; and increase store sales 10% over last month's sales.

Intermediate goals are those which can be achieved within 3 months to a year. Saving for a car down payment or a new computer is an intermediate goal. **Long term goals** take longer than a year to achieve. Purchasing a home or business is a long term goal.

No matter what type of goal you set, they should be **SMART** (specific, measurable, attainable, realistic, and timely).

To achieve a goal it is important to create and write a personal goal statement. This statement helps you understand what the goal is about and why it is important to you.

This process helps you select a time frame and keep focused.

BUDGETS

To achieve our financial goals it is important that we prepare a **budget** which serves as the foundation of any financial plan.

A **budget** is a financial statement written for a future period of time which shows your **income/revenue** (where your money comes from); how much you have; **expenses** (where you money goes); and how to best distribute these funds. A budget helps keep spending under control and helps achieve financial goals.

Personal budgets are very important because they help use keep personal spending under control and allow us to save and reach short term and long term goals. The importance of a budget should be taught at an early age when children start receiving an allowance. Managing money becomes a habit and easily translates into becoming an adult entrepreneur managing a business budget.

STEPS FOR PREPARING A BUDGET

1. List all income or revenue. This includes income from wages or sales (if a business budget) and income from bonuses or investments.

2. List all **fixed expenses** such as rent, mortgages, car payments, insurances, internet, trash, property taxes, etc. These expenses are about the same each month.

3. List **variable expenses** such as groceries, entertainment, and gifts. If budgeting for a business these expenses could be for supplies or employee wages.

4. Calculate the difference between total income and total expenses.

5. Make adjustments if there are more expenses than income which represents a **net loss**.

6. Periodically compare budgeted amounts with the actual amounts. A **spreadsheet** can be used to make this comparison for several months or a year.

Other Types of Financial Statements

- **Income Statement** – A report which shows the revenue and expenses for a period of time. It also shows net income or net loss.

- **Cash Flow Statement** – A report which shows what cash was taken in and what cash was disbursed (paid out). It also shows net cash flow.

- **Balance Sheet** – A report which shows all **assets** (cash, equipment, supplies, and **account receivables** (money owed to your business).The balance sheet also shows all **liabilities** which include **accounts payable** (money you owe to suppliers) and notes payable (money you borrowed). Finally the balance sheet shows **owner's equity** (total assets minus total liabilities).

  Examples of the financial statements are in the appendix in the back of this handbook.

ACTIVITIES/ASSESSMENTS

1. Develop a list of personal short, intermediate, and long term goals.

2. Develop a list of short, intermediate, and long term business goals for operating the school store or some other business.

3. Prepare a personal monthly budget using Excel.

4. Research and list websites which assist in developing budgets and financial statements such as www.mint.com.

5. Students will work in small groups to verify and analyze financial statements from the school store or other place of business, and make recommendations for improving operations.

WRAP-UP

Groups will orally present results of their analysis.

Students may use websites such as Glogster.com to give a visual presentation.

TOPIC 4

BANKING SERVICES

TOPIC 4: BANKING SERVICES

OBJECTIVES: Students will be able to:

- Describe the purpose of a bank
- Investigate and evaluate bank services
- Compute interest
- Access Online banking

ESSENTIAL QUESTION: How do you choose the best bank account?

WARM-UP

How is a budget important to financial planning?

TOPIC 4 HIGHLIGHTS

BANKS PURPOSE

Banks are institutions established for the purpose of holding money for individuals, corporations, and governments. They pay interest for the use of this money. They also loan this money to other individuals, corporations, and governments at a higher rate of interest than they pay to make a profit. They also invest this money in securities.

BANKING SERVICES

Banks today offer services for all your financial transactions. They offer a variety of checking, savings, credit cards, and investment accounts.

- **Checking accounts** enable you to make payments online or using a paper check on bills based on the amount of money you have in your account. You may also make payments using a debit card. This account allows you to use an automatic teller machine (ATM). There are different types of checking accounts some of which pay a small amount of interest. Every check you write should be recorded in a booklet called a **bank register**. Monthly statements are also sent by the bank to show your transactions and any fees charged. Before choosing a checking account you should visit several banks and find the account that best satisfies your needs and offers the lowest service fees.

- **Savings accounts** usually require a minimum balance. Sometimes savings accounts are linked to checking accounts to make it easier to transfer money between the two accounts. The interest the bank pays you for this account varies from bank to bank. Therefore it is good to shop around for the best rate.

- **Money Market Accounts** pay higher rates of interest than savings accounts. However they require a higher minimum balance. There may also be withdrawal restrictions. The interest rate usually varies with the stock market.

- **Certificates of Deposit (CD)** pay the highest rate of interest. However your money must remain in the bank for a long period of time, which could be a

  number of years. There are usually financial penalties for early withdrawal.

- **ATM and Debit Cards** allow you to withdraw money from your checking or savings account without going directly to the bank. Debit cards allow you to pay for store merchandise when shopping. Applications on **smart phones** also allow you to debit your account.

- **Credit Cards** are issued based upon a bank loan or line of credit. The bank charges high interest for the use of this card. Visa, MasterCard, Discovery, and American Express are the most widely used.

- **Investments** usually involve the purchase of securities or stocks and bonds. Stock certificates are issued when a company desires to raise money for expansion. The company goes from being privately held to a public company. Apple, Facebook, General Motors, Google, Nike, and Citicorp all issue stock certificates.

- **ONLINE BANKING**

The internet allows us to do our banking from any location. We no longer need to go to the bank in person or wait in a long line. We can now access our bank accounts from any location, using different electronic devices which have access to the World Wide Web. Pay checks can also be deposited by employers using direct deposit. We can use online bill pay and transfer funds between accounts. There are applications on smart phones which allow us to do banking.

INTEREST

Interest is the cost of using or borrowing money. It is the amount the bank pays you for the use of your money or charges you for lending you money. The amount depends or a rate or percentage which is tied to the financial markets and Federal Reserve Bank.

Interest = Principal x Rate x Time

Example: Calculate the interest paid on a $12,000 loan at 5% for 4 years.

Answer: Interest = 12,000 x .05 x4 = $2,400

ACTIVITIES/ASSESSMENTS

1. Discuss the importance of building a banking relationship with a bank representative.

2. Investigate the types of accounts and interest rates offered at three different banks in your area.

3. Read and analyze a monthly bank statement and determine what fees if any were charged.

4. Complete a bank register.

5. Reconcile the monthly statement and bank register.

Wrap-up: Students will create and present a two minute commercial summarizing this lesson.

TOPIC 5

CREDIT

TOPIC 5: CREDIT

OBJECTIVES: Students will be able to:

- Explain how credit sustains a business.
- Identify the three C's of credit.
- Explain the advantages and disadvantages of capital growth.
- Determine the long term effect of good and bad credit.

ESSENTIAL QUESTION: How do you establish and maintain good credit?

WARM-UP:

1. Compute the interest on a loan of $8600 used to purchase a motorcycle at a 5½% interest rate for 6 years.

2. When is it wise to purchase a certificate of deposit?

TOPIC 5 HIGHLIGHTS

Credit has many definitions. Credit is confidence in a buyer's or borrower's ability to fulfill financial obligations. It can be an arrangement for a person or business to buy goods now and pay later. Credit is the amount placed by a bank at a borrower's disposal. Credit is also payment made on a loan to reduce the amount owed on the loan.

Credit is very important when trying to maintain or grow a business. There are many stories of entrepreneurs who started businesses in their kitchens, garages, and dorm rooms. By using credit these businesses became worth millions of dollars.

Businesses must make important decisions in granting credit to customers and also using credit for large capital investments such as purchasing equipment and **inventory** (goods or product sold).

Credit can sustain or grow a business by increasing sales and giving your business an edge over your competition. There is also risk involved because some customers may not pay on time or not pay at all. Whether a business gives credit or not depends on the type of business and the credit worthiness of the customer. Businesses such as convenience stores and fast food restaurants, do not offer credit to customers. However 95% of sales over the internet are done using credit cards.

When determining who is eligible for credit, one formula known as the **three C's of credit** is used:

1. Character- Does the borrower have an honest reputation?

2. Capacity - Based on borrower's income and expenses, can the borrower repay?

3. Capital – What are the borrower's physical or financial assets or collateral?

More credit is extended to customers with good credit ratings and higher income.

To be competitive a company must always look for new ways to generate revenue by increasing sales. A business must look at current trends and create new products or improve existing products. Many times this means that the business must be expanded and more equipment must be purchased. The money needed to do this expansion is called **growth capital.**

Growing a business requires in depth financial planning based on good record keeping. Usually growth capital is raised using personal savings and borrowing from family, friends, banks and investors.

Capital growth may increase sales and income, but it may also require additional resources such as staff. Therefore the business and owner must maintain good credit.

Activities/Assessments

1. Explain why credit is important to a business and describe some long term good and bad effects credit can have on a business.

2. Research and present factors which determine the level of inventory a business must maintain

Wrap-up: Draw three conclusions from information highlighted in this topic on credit.

TOPIC 6

SAVING AND INVESTING

TOPIC 6: SAVING AND INVESTING

OBJECTIVES: Students will be able to:

- Explain the importance of saving and investing
- Read daily stock reports
- Track investment over several weeks
- Discuss how proper saving and investing can lead to entrepreneurship

ESSENTIAL QUESTION: How does time and risk impact an investment strategy?

WARM-UP:

1. State two definitions of credit.

Identify and explain the 3C's of credit

TOPIC 6 HIGHLIGHTS

Anyone who works and has income will find that much of the money goes to everyday living expenses. These expenses include housing, utilities, food, clothing, and transportation. Although it can be difficult some money should be saved for emergencies. Most financial consultants advise to pay you first no matter how small the amount to get into the habit of saving.

Saving and investing are based on one's long term financial goals. These long term goals could be the purchase of property or a business, children's education, or retirement.

INVESTMENTS

To **invest** money is to commit money for future gain or profit. We commit money to **securities** or accounts which are secured by assets. The three most common types of securities are **stocks**, **bonds**, and **certificates of deposit**. These assets are usually represented by partial ownership in a company or corporation. You hope the value of these securities will increase over time.

The money you invest in a corporation allows it to grow and operate more effectively.

Stocks

As a private company grows, it may need to raise **capital** (money) to expand its facilities and inventory. It may decide to go public and sell shares in the company. To do this they must follow guidelines set by the Securities and Exchange Commission (SEC). These shares or **stock** represent partial ownership or **equity** in a public corporation. General Electric, Ford Motor Company, and Apple are public corporations. When you buy their stock you become part owner. The price of stock tends to change on a daily basis, going up and down. Therefore it is the riskiest type of investment. If the price goes up you make money, and lose money if it goes down. However over the long term they tend to be the best type of investment. When you purchase shares of stock, you become a **stockholder** or **shareholder** and are issued a **stock certificate** representing the number of shares purchased.

Stocks are purchased through brokerage houses or investment banks. Charles Schwab, Edward Jones, and Merrill Lynch are well known investment companies. Stocks may also be purchased at online brokerages such as E*Trade, TD Ameritrade, and Scotttrade.

The price of stock is reported daily on a ticker tape at different exchanges, such as the New York Stock Exchange (NYSE). Its reporting is done on what is referred to as the **Big Board**. Exchanges not only report the current price of stock but also the previous twelve month highest and lowest prices. You want to purchase when the stock price is low and sell when it is high.

What to know before making a stock purchase

Before purchasing stock you must do your homework and learn something about the company and its products or services. You must know its market (who it sells to) and what its cash flow and balance sheet look like. This information can be found in its **annual report**. You should also know what stock analyst predict for the company's future. Also find out if the company recently paid a **dividend** (a portion of the profits) to its shareholders. Dividends are usually paid out quarterly.

Types of Stocks

There are all types of stocks and combinations of stocks. The following represent some of the basic types:

- **Common Stock** is partial ownership in the company

- **Preferred Stock** pays higher dividends than common stock and has voting privileges attached. These shareholders are paid before common shareholders especially if the company goes bankrupt or out of business.

- **Convertible Stocks** are preferred stocks which can be converted to common stocks.

- **Initial Public Offering (IPO)** is first time issued stock to the public to help finance a company's growth.

BONDS

When you purchase a bond you are making a loan to a government or corporation for a period of time (usually 1 to 10 years). This bond has an interest rate and a **maturity date** which tells when the money is due. Bonds are not as risky as stocks and government bonds offer the greatest security. The longer the date to maturity, the higher the interest rate will rise. Bonds make regular interest payments up until they mature. This interest is known as **fixed income**.

Types of Bonds

Bonds differ based on who is issuing the bond, their credit worthiness, maturity date which could be as long as ten years, and interest rate. Interest is usually paid semi-annually. The price of a bond also varies inversely with interest rates. The higher the interest rate the lower the price of bonds. The **Federal Reserve Bank (The Fed)** establishes the prime interest rate which is usually the lowest rate.

Types of Bonds usually available are:

- U.S. Government
- State and municipal
- Mortgage-Backed
- Corporate
- Junk Bonds which have low credit ratings.

Certificates of Deposit

As mentioned previously in Topic 4, **certificates of deposit** are long term savings accounts that pay the highest interest rates and are backed by the Federal Government (FDIC) if the bank should fail. They offer the least risk.

MUTUAL FUNDS

Mutual funds are investments which combine diverse investment vehicles and are held by a group of people who have common financial goals. These funds are watched over by professional money managers. The investors share in the cost and the profits of these accounts. Because these funds are held by a group, there is less risk.

CRYPTOCURRENCY

Cryptocurrency has become a popular and growing investment vehicle within the past several years. Just like other currencies it can be traded and has risk associated with it.

Cryptocurrency is a medium of exchange. We are used to paper and coin currencies such as dollars, euros, yens, pesos, pounds, pennies, etc. **Cryptocurrency** is a form of digital currency mainly used to make purchases over the internet. This monetary system uses complex mathematical algorithms or formulas to create digital tokens. These tokens are transmitted between computers under a secure system. There is also an online accounting system called blockchain to keep track of transactions.

The first and most popular cryptocurrency is Bitcoin It was first introduced in 2009. It is both a payment system and a currency. In early 2017 Bitcoin could be purchased for about $1000. In less than a year, it had risen to $20,000. Many people who purchase cryptocurrency are speculators who invest because they think the price is going to increase.

However, there are no guarantees.

There are now over 4,000 different cryptocurrencies. Litecoin, Ripple, and MintChip are some of the more successful.

DIVERSIFICATION

Most experienced investors have a **portfolio** which contains a variety of stocks, bonds, saving certificates, and mutual funds. They constantly depend on financial experts to track these investments. By diversifying ones portfolio it reduces risk or the chance of losing money.

ACTIVITIES/ASSESSMENTS

1. Select 2 long term financial goals and explain the importance of saving and investing to achieve these goals.

2. Select 3 companies listed on the NYSE and compare and contrast information on their daily stock report.

3. Track these 3 companies for a week and assess if based on their performance they are good or bad

investments at this time.

4. Go online and identify three mutual funds and summarize what type of securities do they invest, and who should invest?

WRAP-UP

Select one of the securities identified in Topic 6 and prepare a two minute commercial to try and sell it to a potential investor.

TOPIC 7

THE BUSINESS PLAN

TOPIC 7: THE BUSINESS PLAN

OBJECTIVES:

- Explain the purpose and importance of a business plan
- Identify and explain the key elements of a business plan
- Create a business plan

ESSENTIAL QUESTION:

How does the development of a sound business plan impact the success of a new business?

WARM-UP:

Develop an argument for portfolio diversification.

TOPIC 7 HIGHLIGHTS

THE BUSINESS PLAN

Once a new entrepreneur has decided on a potential business venture, developing a business plan is crucial to its success. The **business plan** is a document which describes in detail a new business and it operational strategies. It also looks at costs associated with the business and helps discover any problems that may exist when starting up the business.

The business plan is crucial because it is reviewed by potential partners, investors, management, and banks. Thus it is the key document when trying to obtain funding for startup costs.

BUSINESS PLAN COMPONENTS

Developing a business plan requires a great deal of research on all aspects of the new business. The plans real value comes in that it forces the business owner to do research and think thoroughly about the business in a systematic and logical way.

Planning now avoids failure later.

However, most business plans have the following general components.

Executive Summary

This component gives a brief summary of the plan. It should be no more than two pages. It should include a paragraph as to why the business is going to be successful and what is the future outlook for the business and the industry. Statistics and evidence gathered through market research should also be included to support your statements.

Also include a description of the product, the targeted customer, and the owners. If presenting the plan to bankers or investors, include how much money is needed to make the company profitable and how the money will be used. **The executive summary should be written last.**

Company Summary

Identifies the company and gives a concise explanation of the business. It also includes historical information about the business. The location of the business and why the business will succeed is also included.

Products and Services (Marketing Plan)

This section describes the products and services offered by the business as well as future products and services. You should focus on customer benefits. Identify the competition and why your company is better and different. The marketing plan is developed more thoroughly in Topic 8.

Industry Overview

You can find information on your industry by using a search engine (e.g. music recording, jewelry, or fashion design). This section should include industry sales figures in terms of dollars and number of units sold. Any other statistics such as the number of employees should also be included.

Competitor Analysis

The first step in your analysis is to research and identify your competition. This includes your direct competition that make the same product as you and your indirect competition who offer substitute products that will satisfy the customer's needs. In the restaurant industry you have different levels of eat-in restaurants and also fast food restaurants. In the retail industry you have department stores, boutiques, and specialty stores.

In your analysis you should include:

1. Name and location of your competitors

2. Who do they service?

3. What is their product or specialty?

4. How long have they been in business?

5. What is their sales volume?

6. What advantage do you have over your competition?

Operation Plan

The operation plan describes the location of the business and the equipment needed to operate the business. It describes the production process and if any of the production will be outsourced or done by outside vendors or contractors. Who supplies your business should be mentioned in this plan.

Quality safeguards should also be included as well as what procedures will be used to keep cost down and still provide a quality product. When considering the labor supply, how accessible business is to transportation should also be included.

Electronic businesses (E-business) should include a description of the website and how it works and how it will be used. You may also want to mention security safeguards and social networks used.

Organization Plan

This component describes the organization and its structure. It identifies the members of the management team, their qualifications, and position.

A resume for each person should be included as well as a description of their responsibilities in the company. Also include the management philosophy and whether the company is a corporation, partnership, or limited liability.

If there are any partnership agreements, they should also be included.

Financial Plan

The financial plan is a quantitative analysis to determine future profits. This plan helps you prepare your business for the years ahead. If you will need outside funding, this is one of the first sections bankers and investors will review.

The financial plan shows how much money is needed to start and operate the business. It also shows how sales goals will be met.

The financial plan has three main sections:

- Statement of revenue sources and how they will be used indicates the amount of **capital** or money needed to get the business up and running.

- Pro forma financial statements show projections as to when the company will become profitable. It includes a cash flow statement, income statement and a balance sheet. These statements were discussed in Topic 3.

- The third section is a financial analysis which compares your business to the industry standard and indicates a **breakeven point** (point when the revenue equals the expenses).

Growth Plan

Every business needs a plan to grow and stay competitive. Once the business is started what is going to be done to ensure continued growth and profits over many years. What strategies will be used to help the business succeed?

Four strategies investors are interested in are:

- **Product Development** which will include new products or enhancing existing products

- **Market Development** which reaches out to new markets which could be in other countries

- **Market Penetration** which requires selling to more customers or getting customers to buy more of your product.

- **Diversification** involves selling new products in a different market. This is a very risky strategy since you are leaving a market with which you are familiar.

Timing and costs are key factors when deciding on strategy.

Risk Management Plan

In today's economic environment business may not go as we planned. There are financial risks, market risks, time-loss risks, and political risks. Energy costs, change in customer taste, technology innovations, extreme weather conditions are examples of risks.

A successful business identifies their possible risks and develops a strategy plan to operate around these risks.

Having business insurance will minimize these risks.

Plan Layout

I. Cover Page – Include name of company, date name of highest officer, company address, phone, fax number, email, and date.

II. Table of Contents

III. Executive Summary

IV. Company Summary

V. Industry Overview

VI. Competitor Analysis

VII. Operational Plan

VIII. Organizational Plan

IX. Financial Plan

X. Marketing Plan

XI. Growth Plan

XII. Risk Management Plan

XIII. Appendix – Includes financial reports

ACTIVITIES/ASSESSMENTS:

1. Select a business and research and write an industry overview.

2. Identify two well known competitors in the industry and provide a competitor analysis for each.

Wrap-Up

Students should have a two minute discussion on the importance of a business plan.

TOPIC 8

MARKETING

TOPIC 8: MARKETING

OBJECTIVES: Students will be able to:

- Layout and evaluate a marketing plan
- Discuss the impact of false advertising on a business

ESSENTIAL QUESTION: How does a good marketing strategy impact a business?

WARM-UP:

Identify and explain two components of a business plan.

Topic Highlights

Definition

The American Marketing Association defines **marketing** as an activity, set of institutions, and processes for creating, communicating, delivering, and exchanging offerings that have value for customers, clients, partners, and society. This is not the only definition. Because the way business is conducted is ever- changing, the definition of marketing is ever-evolving. Marketing is used to identify, satisfy, and keep the customer

Marketing management is a major component in any business management program. Today many universities view it as a science because in dealing with the issue of selling to a customer companies must design a plan that uses psychology, sociology, mathematics, economics, statistics, and a few other sciences.

  Thus it is a major component in an entrepreneurship program. How are items marketed in the school store or sports concession stand so as to increase sales, product awareness, customer satisfaction, and repeat customers?

Marketing Objectives are the results a company wants to accomplish through its marketing campaign. The objectives for a new business should be clear, concise, measurable, and easily controlled.

When listing these objectives they should include the following:

- Introduction of the new product or enhancements and innovations to existing product.
- An organizational description of the team.
- Projected sales or market share
- Projected profits
- How the product or service will be priced
- What are the distribution channels? These include delivery terms, shipping, receiving, handling, storage, and warehousing.
- Advertising (media or print)

Marketing Orientation and Strategies

Market orientation refers to the way a company feels

about its product or service. **Market strategies** are plans of action for getting the product or service to the consumer. **Market mix** refers to a combination of strategies used to reach the consumer.

Over the years marketing orientation or the way a company feels about its product has changed. In the early years marketing focused on one of the following orientations:

- Production – Company produces as much as possible because of high demand for the product. An example is car production in the late 1940's and 1950's.

- Product - Company focuses on producing a quality product because consumer has high standards. Luxury cars, watches and handbags are examples.

- Selling – Company tries to sell as much as possible using varies promotion techniques. This is used when a product is in high demand. A good example of this strategy is lower priced pizza and televisions at the start of the football season.

Recent approaches in market orientation focus on the needs and tastes of the consumer. These approaches use market research. They also use Research and Development (R&D) to create new and improved products.

A few of these approaches include:

- Relationship Marketing- maintaining good customer relationships

- Business Marketing – focus is selling to other businesses

- Social Marketing – there is a benefit to the whole society

- Internet Marketing- marketing via email, online, search engine, desktop, and affiliate, and QR codes or Quick Response codes.

Marketing Strategies are long term or multiple year plans for dealing with the development and growth of a product. Earlier strategies consisted of the 4P's; product, place, price, and promotion. In recent years a fifth P has emerged which deals with people. Some strategies deal with market dominance, product differentiation, and how innovative is the product. Many times a company may use a combination of these strategies called a **market mix**.

Today online marketing strategies enable businesses to quickly reach a larger market. Social media such as Twitter, Tumblr, Facebook, Pinterest and Instagram can have a major impact on sales because of their global audience.

Marketing Plans are one of the foundations for having a successful business. It is the plan used to accomplish marketing objectives, reach the target market or customer, and grow the business.

The market plan is developed based on market research and if developed properly can be used to convince investors and banks to help provide funding.

Market Plan Components consist of the following:

- Executive Summary – focuses on marketing objectives, budget, and business projections.

- Business Overview – gives information on the state of industry, competitors, strengths, and weaknesses of the industry.

- Target Market – profiles the customer who will purchase product.

- Marketing Objectives - identifies the goals or what the plan is to accomplish.

- Tactics or Action Plan – states how the business will be advertised over a given time frame.

- Market Strategies – gives the mix of strategies that will be used to meet objectives. It also identifies the tasks that must be completed and identifies who is responsible for each task.

- Budget – gives the cost of operating the business and the anticipated revenue.

Activities/Assessments

1. Research and identify several marketing strategies that are popular today.

2. Identify an online strategy that is used and companies who use it.

3. Explain the 5P's of marketing.

Wrap-up:

Summarize a component of a marketing plan

Appendices

A Personal Monthly Budget

B Sample Consolidated Balance Sheet

C Sample Monthly Income Statement

D Sample Monthly Statement of Cash Flows

Appendix A

Personal Monthly Budget

Month_____ Year

INCOME:
Wages/Tips	$ 5,280.00
Interest income	$ 2.00
Other Income	$ 250.00
Total Income	**$ 5,532.00**

EXPENSES:
Savings	$ 200.00
Rent/Mortgage	$ 1,670.00
Health Insurance	$ 320.00
Car Payment	$ 360.00
Car Insurance	$ 225.00
Utilities	$ 230.00
Phone	$ 146.00
Cable	$ 87.00
Credit Cards/Store Accounts	$ 180.00
School Loans	$ 260.00
Groceries	$ 400.00
Transportation/Gas	$ 230.00
Laundry/Cleaners	$ 128.00
Clothing/Hair Allowance	$ 225.00
Entertainment	$ 240.00
Gifts	$ 5.00
Other Expenses	$ 200.00
Total Expenses	**$ 5,106.00**
NET INCOME	**$ 426.00**

Appendix B

Easy Corporation

Consolidated Balance Sheet

December 31, 20__

Assets

Current Assets:		
Cash or Cash Equivalents	$40,750	
Accounts and notes receivables	68,500	
Inventories at lower of cost	91,750	
Prepaid expenses	7,000	
Total current assets		$208,000
Investments:		
Bonds	42,250	
Dividends from stocks	24,000	
Total Investments		$ 66,250
Fixed Assets:		
Land	25,000	
Buildings	92,000	
Machinery and equipment	199,820	
Total Fixed Assets		$316,200
Intangible Assets:		
Goodwill		$55,000
Total Assets		$645,450

Liabilities

Current Liabilities:		
Accounts Payable	$ 63,284	
Income Tax Payable	14,666	
Dividends Payable	5,000	
Accrued l Liabilities	9,410	
Total Current Liabilities		$92,360
Long-term Liabilities:		
Bonds Payable	$34,000	
Total Long-term Liabilities		$34,000
Deferred income taxes payable		$7,790
Total Liabilities		$134,150
Stockholders' Equity		$511,300
Total Liabilities and Stockholders' Equity		$645,450

Appendix C

XYZ Travel Service

Income Statement

For the Month Ended October 31, 2012

Fees earned		$8,300.00
Expenses:		
Wages expense	$3,725.00	
Rent expense	1,450.00	
Utilities expense	980.00	
Supplies Expense	875.00	
Miscellaneous expense	640.00	
Total expenses		7,670.00
Net income		$ 630.00

Appendix D

XYZ Travel Service

Statement of Cash Flows

For the Month Ended October 31, 2012

Cash flows from operating activities:		
Cash received from customers	$8,300.00	
Deduct cash payments for expenses and		
payments to creditors	7,740.00	
Net cash flows from operating activities		$ 560.00
Cash flows from investing activities:		
Cash payments for purchase of building		(32,000.00)
Cash flows from financing activities:		
Cash received from issuing stock	40,000.00	
Deduct cash dividends	2,600.00	
Net cash flows from financing activities		37,400.00
Net cash flow and October 31, 2012 cash balance		$5,960.00